CITY BIRD

Also by Arlene Weiner
Escape Velocity

CITY BIRD

Poems by
Arlene Weiner

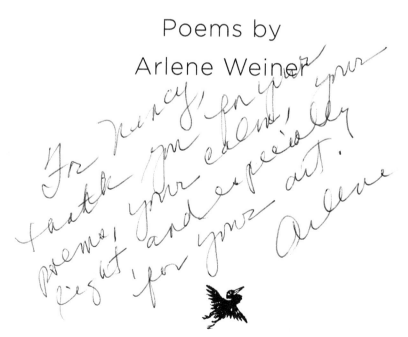

RAGGED SKY PRESS · PRINCETON · NEW JERSEY

Published by Ragged Sky Press
270 Griggs Drive, Princeton, NJ 08540
www.raggedsky.com

Library of Congress Control Number: 2016935593

ISBN 978-1-933974-21-7

Cover design: Dirk Rowntree

Book design: Jean Foos
          CargoCollective.com/FoosDesign

Cover illustration by Rose Gauss ©2009; RoseGauss.com,
          TheDrawPage.com

Fonts: Gotham and Mercury

Printed in the United States of America

First Edition

With gratitude to the many friends and friends of poetry who have encouraged and supported me, and especially to Michael Wurster and Ellen Foos; to the members of the poetry workshops I've attended, including Pittsburgh Poetry Exchange, U.S. 1 Poets' Cooperative, Squirrel Hill Poets, Madwomen, and Mike Schneider's East End Poets; and to Rob. And to my mother, who introduced me to poetry and who writes poems for family occasions.

Contents

One

Two

Three

Four

Five

Six

ONE

In Dreams I Ride a Bus

Because a bus is a house of many windows
Because it carries light through dark streets
and shade through hot streets

Because it is safety between
the sadness of work
and the sadness of home

Because it embraces strangers' privacies
where the woman driving
chats with a child-sized woman behind her

a woman with pony-pied skin
rubs scented oil into blue gums
the pierced girl gives me a seat

Because it arrives or never arrives

Inwood Journey

(near Dyckman Street, New York City)

Go through a keyhole-shaped court:
to your left and right
flecked with black and white
stone steps where ruled
an older girl playing teacher
still sharp and cold.

The clown nose of the king's face
on the glass-paned door
has vanished, a hole
in its place. The scrolled
backplate with its wry mouth
that seemed to cry
is tarnished.

A floor of six-sided tiles
dulled by dust.
Wood covers the inner door.
The hall, fluorescent-lit,
suggests night and distrust.
The stairs, white stone green-veined,
slump in the middle. Up one flight,

five doors don't let you in.
But doesn't a girl within
hear a call? *Mira, mira.*
She leans out on a wide sill,
stretches up, watches new flakes fly:
black against the white sky,
bright against the dark opposing wall.

Little Dancer

I saw Degas' little dancer
playing Frisbee in the street.
Bronze, she leaned backward
as in an embrace
or eluding embrace,
her stance not bronze
but a pause in flow—
seized disc from the air,
spun it away, danced *Yes!*—
celebrated herself
with herky-jerky hips.

Flamenco Dancer in White

Oh, my girl, city bird, when I see you stand
above the others, head high, skirts high,
I believe you're beautiful. You're ready
to stamp your heels, swirl, leaving behind
the gray day, when you peck peck peck,
head down, on the gray street for bread.
You're not pretty, city bird, you're like me, pure
as city snow. Now spine straight, neck long,
for a minute you belong above the others.
Stretch upward, assured—fly.
City bird, dance for us, who keep our heads low,
dance more furiously than falling city snow.

At Spuyten Duyvil

My brother stood many an hour
to watch and name the trains
where they crossed the Harlem River
the powerful diesel engines
the long countable freights
the slender silver cars
from places we'd never been
and never expected to see

He left our dim neighborhood
lived decades in green New Jersey
behind the basalt Palisades
then crossed the Hudson again
lives east of the Tappan Zee
the long long Tappan Zee bridge
the slow-moving tolled bridge

You're moving closer
to where we came from

A joke—he's moved always
upward, upward
It's true he can take a train south
a convenient commuter train
past the perilous neighborhood
where both of us began
and where on restless nights
I'm lost in a tangle of streets

That train doesn't stop
in our old neighborhood
but one Sunday at Spuyten Duyvil
the silver beautiful train
lay a stiff broken arc
and some of the lucky commuters
who sped through that neighborhood
stopped short at the Harlem River
and will not cross again

Weegee the Famous

A man's lost his hat.
Brass buttons in charge.

The widow's mouth and the prostitute's
are black Os.

Weegee carries a high-heeled shoe,
a teddy bear, to toss on the street.

Even at the beach
his flash calls up night.

Hansi's Memory

While she dresses for the morning, pulling up
the plain heavy stockings, fastening clasps at the thigh,
stepping into a slip, she hears the old man praying
the morning prayers in the next room.

On Ellwood Street two-bladed seeds
spin to the ground from the green
trees. Her steps click quickly.
Quiet dusky morning, a few cats, the girl
with white hair and lashes standing in shadow.

In late spring in Hungary, trees shook
golden powder from fine brushes, stood
as if in circles of lamplight. The scent recalled
her mother's powder when she dressed for evening.

The old couple who rent her a room call her Hansi also.
Last Sunday their granddaughter wore
a seed on the bridge of her nose
and came to Hansi's room for dark chocolates.

A life in one room. A job in the dusk
of a yarn store, halfway down the subway steps,
among women. Chatter of needles,
brilliant colors of yarn. Safety.

Next month for remembrance
she will light candles for her mother
and father together, as they lived
and may have died. She knows not when, how.

The trees gone now from Ellwood Street.
I knit a shawl of comfort, a story.
I give Hansi a husband in a topcoat,
no children, for Hansi was delicate.

In Junior High School I Was Voted Most Cheerful

Before we made the transition
to high school, sex, ambition,
before I grew long hair
and men in the library stacks
began whispering in my ear
before I put myself in my pocket,
carried myself like a matchbook
to light the jack-o'-lantern
math teacher and my father's friends,
then, I was Most Cheerful. Claude
was Smartest and Wittiest both,
the one boy who didn't giggle
when in science I announced
I would demonstrate the fourth
of the six simple machines,
the Screw. Ellen was Best Dressed,
Alan was Handsomest,
and I was Most Cheerful, that year.

By the Sink

Mother stood Daughter on a chair,
gave her a little knife
and a bunch of bitter roots
like red clown noses.
Showed how to scrub them, slice
the ends off, cut their tips
round and around,
then drop them in cold water.
Those cuts would open then
like lids or lips.

A female art:
sharp blade, sharp chill,
made sharp-tasting dolls' hearts
into radish roses.

Diane Arbus, *Two Ladies at the Automat, N.Y.C. 1966*

I'd shared their table a few years before.
The one in the leopard-skin hat
had asked the other, *Where
did you do it the first time?* Green
as I was, I knew what *it* was from the answer:
Under the boardwalk on the Island.

I was eating Horn & Hardart's
baked macaroni and cheese. The Automat
looked out onto Bryant Park, in those days
not a place I felt safe unless with a boy,
or a couple of boys. *That first time
I did it for free.* I can still call up
the Automat's inviting array of foodstuffs
sleeping behind small glass doors,
available to anyone for a few quarters,
can call up the oval dish,
the soft custard, its browned top.

One put out her cigarette, said,
*I have an appointment in an office
at 3 o'clock. One of my weeklies.*

I already knew that "the Island"
didn't always mean Coney Island, I already
had sat at a table in the great public library
across the park, a long table with green-shaded lamps,
had seen the catalogue
of thousands and thousands of books,
had chosen, given an order, had been served
my choice from its hidden inexhaustible treasury.

The baked macaroni and cheese was delicious and cheap.
Oh ladies! One of you may still be living,
or both. I hope you landed soft.
In Bryant Park on the monument to Bryant,
almost hidden, his lines about eddying dust.

Tontine

I don't suppose that if you were a Borgia
you'd join a family tontine:

a scheme where each one antes
and the last to die takes the whole pot.

My mother's the winner of this kind of lottery:
The last of five sisters and brothers,

eighteen first cousins,
and so the last to sweep together

the memorial hoard of gold and grit,
cigar bands, needles, pennies, buttons.

Last to mourn Charlie who walked away
and was never heard from again,

Dorothy, who died in her teens. Last to have seen
my grandmother's tears falling into the soup she stirred.

Last to remember her dark-haired and plump,
the scorched sweet scent of her daily baking.

And who after me will recall my mother
knocking the inside of her wrist against her hip

or leaning into the living-room doorway singing,
making an entrance like a showgirl?

Parking Parallel, for a Friend Whose Work Has Come to Nothing

Tight spot, busy narrow street,
behind a pickup truck, wide.
Stop anyway, line up, go into reverse—
traffic behind me pressing: *hurry.*
Turn the wheel hard, hard,
inch back, swing out,
slow and worried,

glance up: guy idling
high on the library steps
gestures with both hands,
twist, twist, come on, come on.
Finish cleanly at the curb,
no scrape or bump,
step out, lock up—
wave at my fan: *Olé!*

Two

At the Coffee Tree

Black brows over bedroom eyes. Dark
stubble on cheeks at four o'clock,
clean line shaved at your white nape.
I recognize you, Handsome, your type:
trouble. No laptop, no book,
just giving your cup of joe a deep look.

Handsome is as handsome does.
Lost father, lover, are you phoning someone
or postponing the first drink of the day?
The loneness of you pulls me as I think
it pulled my great-grandmother,
my aunt, my son's mother-in-law.
And, yes, the blue eyes.

There was Johnny Ryan and Johnny O'Brien,
John Dwyer and John Burke.
A line of dark horses, pieces of work,
soldiers of misfortune.
One took to the road and one to drink,
one killed on the rails, one went
for a soldier and came back bent.

Finished now, you pick up your phone,
struggle out of the tall chair.
I see one of your sandals is high built,
a cothurnus—your injury possibly lifelong.
Forgive my severity, Pierced-Foot.
I hope you're going to an interview, a date,
some new luck, not to chronic disappointment
or chthonic appointment with Fate.

The Lois and Clark Expedition

They didn't have an Indian guide.
They started out from Metropolis,
went west, stayed at tourist cabins.
Clark drove so slowly.
But somehow while she was sleeping
they covered distance.

He had an unerring sense of direction,
as if road turnings were signposted.
The sex was good, in a vanilla way.
He wouldn't play rough.
She wished he'd use contact lenses
or grow a beard, but he refused.

Sometimes she thought, *Did I settle?*
The Rockies exhausted her.
She lost hope. But they kept going.
Later on, there were absences and excuses.
Locked cupboards. She overlooked them.
They'd come so far. And winter was setting in.

Experiment in Living

Not as a man, but like a man:
in a one-room cabin
with pegs where I'd hang
five shirts, two pairs of pants.

A peacoat, watch cap. Boots and galoshes
by the door. A dog leash.
Curtainless windows and certainly
no ruffled pillows piled on the bed.

Worktable on trestles. By accident
of schooling I already know
Phillips-head screwdriver,
ball-peen hammer, rip and crosscut saw.

I'll have a power saw too, power drill,
make a kitchen shelf for an assortment of cans,
black beans and WD-40 among them,
put up a pendulum clock. Spend my money
on a weather station and high octane.

And like a man, I'll write a book about it,
Where I Went and Why I Went There,
Seven Steps to the Simple Life,
or What I Think and Feel and Why You Should Care.

Two Stories

In the heimisch Swiss barometer
the Mr. and Mrs. don't seem to have a home life.
When she's in he's out. When she's out he's in.
They smile, whatever the pressure.
Maybe in the woodcarver's shop
he heard a call, *cuckoo, cuckoo*
and was pained, thinking the jibe was for him.

When I looked for a place apart from my husband
I took him with me. He was silent
about the choice, not to put a thumb on the scale.
I turned down the spiffy condos
for a brown house with a chickadee
buzzing in the shrubs, two stories, green shutters,
a roof of overlapping slates.

It looked more like a child's picture
of a house than anywhere I'd lived.
When I rented that one he said
I'd have to bake gingerbread
for the neighbor children, a good witch.

The Swiss know a trick to balance
enmity with peace. Once we'd had dinner
in Biel/Bienne on the exact line
where French and German meet.
Enormous alpenhorns on the wall,
a German menu and a sour remark
about the two kids playing some kind of pinball
and exclaiming "Merde!"
They were *from across the road.*

After three years my husband helped me load the car
with everything a moving van couldn't take,
and I moved back. Now the pressure's off,
we share silences, talk about the cat.
Today a chickadee visited our rhododendron
and I called him to see it, a returnee
after a summer away. It looked, head cocked,
at our hanging plant as if, small-brained as it was,
it remembered the winter feeder.

Second-Hand Hat

For four days I've shoveled snow
more than daily, down to the white footprints
of those who've already passed.
Today I'm wearing the hat
that my niece gave to my mother,
my mother passed to my daughter
and my daughter left me, still in its box.
It has fake-fur-lined earlaps
and looks good for invading Moscow—
and only that.

The scrape of blade on walk
takes me back to the great blizzard
when my father stayed home from work,
so that ever after the grate
of metal on sidewalk woke me
to hope for a holiday,
riding my Flexible Flyer,
gliding smooth until we encountered
such "holidays" as I'm making,
cleared spaces where runners caught,
the sled shuddered, while his strength
pulled me through them.

I'm getting the knack of shoveling:
a good blade, not bent, wielded soon enough
so that the snow's untrodden,
straight ahead on the narrow path.
strokes side to side where the walk is wide.
On the lawn, varves of compacted flakes,
icicle melt, down, fleece, dog piss,
chronicle of sediments and catastrophes.
Where is the rabbit that I saw in my yard
evenings, into November?

Where is the pink hat I wore
when we stood by a snow-covered lake
and smiled for the camera?
I'll dig it out, put it on and we'll walk
in the thin logged-over woods
gliding through scrapes,
sliding down scarps
where the Bible rock, an erratic,
marks our accustomed trail.

Beatitude

God bless the men with the skill to plumb
our plugged-up plumbing and see without shock
our clogs our crud our clumped hair
and the women too, though in my life men.
Bless them who know what's what
when unscrewing or screwing,
who have tools that fit heads,
who neatly put blade into slot,
who overlook our dumb work,
the scratched surfaces, stripped threads.
The patient ones with the will to spend hours
stripping layers of old stuff
to get down to grain
and then carefully wash the brush,
those whose shims make the loose firm
those who get the stuck unstuck
those who come in the cold to get the heat on

and bless especially those who come
when they're called or at least
call back and honestly say they can't come.

Men's Watches

Men used to wear
watches they had to wind.
On the wrist,
or kept near the chest
and taken out
ceremoniously.

Sometimes they'd find
their watch slow
or fast, or it stopped.
Shaking might make
it run again,
or the heat of the hand.

After repair
they'd check it
often, quickly,
not only when they
wanted the time.

When a wife has an affair
or loses a breast
her husband looks
at her sidelong,
thinks of her
again and again
while at work.

That wears off
if she keeps ticking
the old way.

Glove Song

I've lost my glove, my good,
my green glove,
that matched my coat so well,
and where will I get another?
Go to the store, there's plenty more.

I've lost my green glove, suede,
that I wore so often, made
part of myself, nights and cold mornings
and when will I get another?
Be it greener than moss, loss is loss.

I've lost my green suede glove,
dear to me, almost loved
and who will get me another?
You might have thought, before you bought.

I've lost my dear, my green, my good, my suede glove,
that matched my coat so well and not less dear
because bought cheap, the last in the store
and out of season.
How will I do in the cold, in my old coat
with no gloves?
Without a match, you must pinch and patch.

Ah, I've found my dear, my green, my suede glove,
my good, that I treated so badly, dropped
more than once, stepped on
and now think highly of—
my suede, my dear, my green glove.
Is it so dear, love? Now you've a pair,
take care, take care.
Take more care.

Like Love

Once, on a woodland path, you saw a toad
and pointed it out to the children. They shouted,
Catch it! Catch it! You tried, but were empty-handed,
covered the place in the road
                where it had been.

Then I, not quick of hand or eye—
who'd never pounded fist into mitt, waiting
to make a game-saving quick stop
or breathtaking stretch and reach, *I*
                          got it!—

stepped up and covered it on my first try.
That was a lesson. To catch
the slow, large, warty, skeptical thing
you have to want
                to catch it,

be willing
          to hold it.

Making Loaves

Get a starter with life in it.
Keep it covered.
Feed it often.

The black mother will rise
and fill the kitchen with her tang
even before a match is struck.

Stir. Sift flour, to strain out impurities,
agglutinations,
with a little sugar,
enough salt.

Mix all.
Let the mass rest.

Turn it onto the old board,
fold, press, fold again,
beat the muscular round with your fist
until it springs back from your touch.

Resistance, compliance.
Divide into loaves, let rest once more.
When you have done this again and again
you won't need measure,

you'll move in a cloud
of spores like souls, wild yeasts,
perfume your loaves
with your own particular scent.

Waltz for My Husband

My dear, we're dancing in the photo
that's stuck in the mirror frame.
I'm not turned to you, I'm smiling,
I grant you, at the photographer.

The photographer was young
the occasion a wedding, a reunion,
the hard times almost behind us:
our bereavements, your abandonment.

A feast snatched from the wolf
the black familiar wolf waiting
outside the cleared space
in the familiar dead dark.

The wolf with soft black fur...
No yellow eyes would shut
No yellowing teeth covered and harmless
unless I would say the charm.

Oh my dear here's your charm then:
I will not turn away from your fire
I will not die and leave you free
to go to the wolf, unburdened of me.

My Old Father among Women

blunt knife among spoons
they reflect him plumped and shining
as he was   as he was

the blade and the bowl, the blade and the bowl

and among men   the vain little match I was
saw warty Jack kindle and grin
when I got on the bus
as I was   as I was

the match and the candle, the match and the candle

and you a boy   jumped and smiled
by the water   by the water
as we were   as we were

the wave and the beach   the beach and the wave

Reading Du Fu While My Husband Is in China

A hummingbird has already visited the garden.
Like your wife, I observe the change in seasons
and must prepare my husband's clothes.

Tomorrow there will be an eclipse of the sun.
He may see it in the morning,
our son in the evening, I not at all.

I don't worry that he won't return.
He will ride Dragonair to Hong Kong.
We exchange e-mail daily.

Last night I tied five bundles of prunings,
carried them in my arms to the curb,
medieval serf gathering fuel.

Your wife beat the laundry against a stone.
You imagined her wishing the beat of her club
would travel across your separation.

My husband visited your thatched cottage.
Does the river still bend there?
Is the air sweet?

Sustainability, a Love Poem

I read of a green couple in Vancouver
who resolved to live on local produce, grown
within a hundred miles.
So soon they were starving, forced to cheat,
include trucked-in wheat.
I wake up beside you thinking,
here in our own
cold climate and no seacoast
what could we live on?

My grapefruit disappears from the breakfast plate
and your orange. The bread
is close-grained and gray. There's no coffee.
I'll look for blue flowers in summer,
dig up chicory root and roast it,
make cornmeal pancakes
with syrup: maple or corn.
There are no olives, oysters, salmon,
but you can bring in a string
of trout. We pass up squirrels and squab,
try dried deer meat, fat of a hog fed on cobs and acorns.

The hard kind of squash, best after frost,
for suppers in winter; dried corn, root vegetables.
Goat's cheese, beans and, in season, greens.
In spring we'll hunt fiddleheads, eagerly grub
dandelions from the lawn.
We'll plant peaches and plums,
learn to love elderberries and mulberries,
make a poor sort of wine
but good moonshine.

You'll permit yourself Connecticut tobacco.
For sweetness, we'll boil beets, keep bees.
We'll have beeswax candles then, and sunlight
that comes millions of miles
at its own expense.

Laundry

I peel your black socks
off my cotton shirt warm from the dryer,
think of Katherine Hepburn
picking leeches off Bogart
in *The African Queen.*

So many of them! She starchy,
and I starchily think, so many
black socks and not all alike—
they require meticulous matching.
I hold each to natural light

to discern ribs and clocks.
I fold your white laundry and pack
T-shirts, briefs, socks
into your dresser
so many! and only a short stack

of mine. But when I said I was blue
you took a break to brew good black
coffee. Your socks can cling where they like.
Tonight I'll finger your ribs,
peel the shirt off your back.

My Husband Buys Cheese at Pennsylvania Macaroni Co.

My favorite's semi-soft, split by a layer of ash.
Not mold. Melting indulgence, penance, melting again.
At our wedding he smashed
a flash bulb in place of the traditional glass
while uncles shouted encouragements, traditionally crass.

Even the name, Morbier, smacks of death.
Maybe it's Basque.
The aisle that leads to the altar is lined with *crash*.
Volcanic soils are fertile, so after eruptions
people repeople the slippery scree.

Weddings were about repeopling then,
the community-approved means of production.
Kauai was paradise though damaged by Iniki.
An old discursive cookbook says, *What a friend
we have in cheeses.*

I think we'll go together to the end.
Morbier is edible, even to the rind.

Three

The Mother

I could have lifted the girl alone,
gurney to table, so light. Her age on the chart,
nineteen. The requisitioned test:

a rhythm strip, tracing of the heart.
Contorted, contracted, her hollow chest
didn't allow the usual placements.

As I felt for my landmarks of bone
I noticed her fingernails, little works of art,
sparkly, in three tones.

The door opened before I had time
to start the EKG. *I'm*
the mother, announced the made-up face

in the opening. How many times in such places
had someone leaned
out of a doorway and asked *Where*

is the mother? Irregular as it was,
inconvenient, I made room for the mother
in my small space.

The Kid

The hospital elevators traveled in pairs
like police in bad neighborhoods.
A panel showed the floors they were on.
People watched it like off-track bettors,
grumbled companionably,
struck up lifetime friendships.

Visiting hours had started.
A little crowd had gathered
as if at a bus stop.

The second thing I noticed about the kid
was his red hair—*Carrot-top*
would be his nickname
if he had a nickname—
because the first thing I noticed
was his baby arms: their whole length
only the length of my forearms.
Twenty years old.

We'd all been waiting a little while
when he came up
and we continued to wait.
Carrot-top began to grumble:
These elevators are such a pain!
They ought to fix them, they ought
to get a better system.

It seemed a routine, cheerful somehow, rote.
Some of us smiled, but nobody spoke.
Nobody else felt qualified to complain.

Seconds and Irregulars

instruct me in perfection.
How many ways
things go awry. Take
for example these simple
sheets. One color's misprinted,
the sky-blue, the pattern
everywhere askew. Or
stripes mismatched,
embellished hem
sewn to the long edge,
corner seams taped
on the brighter side,
now the wrong side.

All these still usable.
We don't see
the worst errors—
they're shredded or sent
to a charity for refugees—
weren't these made
in the Third World anyway?

Soft bed.
Clean sheets: I smooth them,
draw them taut.

Every fair from fair
sometime declines.

A Double-Wide in Virginia

I'm at my cousin's. She is sleeping.
Near 70, she said, *I'm nine months pregnant,*
laughed. Big-bellied with tumors.
Sealed in our flesh, not a covenant,
as with men, but a damaged spiral
that turns our female flesh against us,
seeds breast or womb with too much bloom.

Our great-grandfather sat
on his shabby broad-armed chair as on a throne
and took us, two little girls, by our thin wrists.
He could sleep with open eyes,
for he was blind, like a god.
Evenings he called for schnapps,
sang, *Zip zoop, flaysh is tier.*
Sip soup, meat's expensive. Dear flesh.

Origins, old allegiance, drew me here.
We were playmates. A cabinet,
from our grandmother's apartment,
carved deeply in a Jacobean design,
stacked urns and scrolls, banners,
like an old bookplate, was a hand-me-down
fifty or sixty years ago, from rich relations.

No rich relations between us for years.
Silences, distance. The scarred cabinet
was not much tended. She sleeps a great deal.
Coughs. After this morning's sleep,
she woke and asked, *Did you see any deer?*

No. I saw birds, but no deer.
I saw great graceful birds, black,
spiral in cold morning air,
the shallow v of vultures, late risers.
I think she sleeps more and more.
Life is a dream, great-grandmother sang in Yiddish
in her last bed. Our great-grandfather: *Flesh is dear.*

To John in the ICU

Scolding never moved you, or moved you
in the opposite direction.
Redheaded, quick, nicknamed Matchstick,
you were blamed for the neighbors' transgressions.
Maybe it was the smile you could never quite quench.
Now we're exasperated: it was careless
to let your lungs collapse, you're taking so much time
starting to breathe again and you won't, won't, won't
come when we call, busy yourself with what we think
is important, the ins and outs of rib, air,
urine, blood. You were never lazy—it's time
to shuck the sloth, shake the lead hand off,
wink, tell us it was a tease, faking, infuriate us. *Please.*

Comfort Zone

They come after work
through sugar-white snow falling
pink under anti-crime lights, sit

in this room under water.
They keep it light, laugh while he floats
over their talk like the fluorescent fixture.

A capable man on a ladder
last Saturday fixing a basement light
when his wife heard…

she turns from the memory, returns, returns.
He lay on the cellar floor, out like—
shattered. In induced coma now,

damaged. He hovers, their hopes hover,
in the shadowless light of the family
waiting room.

Whether his light is quite out, whether
his hands will grasp, move, whether
he'll return with speech, memory—fixed—

how much? they don't ask. *He's
in capable hands,* they say, *Hey, leave
some of that pizza,* step out to light cigarettes,

tell stories smoothed like rosary beads—
*Remember the time the lights went out
during the Super Bowl?* that show him
in a good light. Absurd. Furious. Whole.

Line of Beauty

The young fellow
took off the dressing, said with feeling,
It's beautiful.
Three days after surgery, my incision
straight, already healing.
He left me undressed.

Twelve days after surgery,
my PCP looked, said, *It's beautiful.*
Explained, *If you've ever seen*
hip surgery,
its brute force.

I've submitted to the knife before:
legs stripped, womb taken,
a chunk of back punished
for harboring promiscuous cells.
This is a new thrill: an insertion.

Maybe I'll get a bikini for exhibition
of my best part, the surgeon's art.
I won't count on it, with sutures
still in. An infection can spell ruin,
or looseness about some prohibition:

crossing my legs, bending too far.
Now it's a thin red line. In the future
I'll make it a scar.

Edge

Because his wife asked, the grandfather
wields edger and weed-whip, watches
the blurred filament fell the tall grass.

She is Catholic, knows suffering
and hope twine. Her hoe and trowel scrape
mud from the flooded tender annuals
in tidy beds.

There was a storm, the power failing,
limbs falling, three nights ago, the night
they heard the doctors say, *Inoperable.*

She tips water from saucers, digs weeds,
prunes heavily to set all to rights.
Her hostas spread broad leaves
unmarred by snails. Scape and stalk rise.

A cardinal hides its red in the shrub,
a robin sings and sings from high.
Daylilies—their neighbor calls them
firecracker flowers—point
small fingers to the sky.
She hasn't seen a firefly.

Their granddaughter will not see a firefly,
a bee, the dreadful congregation
of turkey buzzards around an opened deer.

To be consoled that she is safe
from wasp and coiled snake,
from traitor and thief,
that she will not coarsen
or know their grief, would be cold.

The grandfather gets the chainsaw,
fills it with gasoline
from the red safety container,
thinks of flame, of a vapor trail igniting,
to burn, rush, burst out.
Red, red, red, red, red!

He closes the can with care,
yanks the starter cord,
lets the roaring chain speak.
The saw chews through green limbs.

His old arms' strength knots.
Again. Again. Chunks drop to the ground,
fresh leaves. He lops slender trunks, storm-downed,
into lengths to fit the hearth for their winter fire.

Skyfall

A marathoner breasting the tape then collapsing,
David died the first day of the year.
Cerebral accident at the last, as at his birth.
He'd achieved eighty years, a milepost
a lot of us won't reach.

My grocery sack must weigh twenty pounds
with the library book I added.
I carry it over my shoulder,
so I creep like a hunchback over ice
packed down from December's snow.

On David's birthday his sister took him to dinner
and the latest Bond movie, *Skyfall*.
Action, girls, hardly any talking.
He asked her afterward, *How*
did you know I'd like it?

Two years of chemo, light as a leaf,
shuffling, unable to pick up his feet.
Her burden put down after years of care,
she cries. At home, I rub my wrist,
unpack, take out the book, by a doctor: *How We Die*.

On the Way from St. Scholastica's Church to Calvary Cemetery I Think of an Astronaut

A man goes into space. His twin
remains on the spinning earth.

Under the high stone bridge,
avenue of body shops, redemption centers,
animal rescue league,
a tire store's come-hither display,
15-foot inflated Gumby,
bobs and bows.

Short-armed, it crassly rhymes
with the Man fixed to the cross.
Is this the place of the bad love:
weak love, strong love of wrong,
love too material or insufficient?

Send me some charm to turn
curdled whey to wine. Call it grace.
Send some animal rescue to warm
the weathered men with burdens

of bottles and cans, to feed the strays,
to see the disappointed,
the insufficient, to bring them home.

The man in space swings above us, an eye.

Lessens

Look back and your idol's name
has an asterisk in the record book.

Your first crush had a risible hairdo
and visible streaked makeup.

That doesn't mean you should
have buyer's remorse.

The moon colony shut down
but you computed an arc tangent, cashed out.

The guy who gave back his medals
pedals ahead of you in your furious cycles.

The author whose depleted fame spurred you
to emulation has lines that stir you still.

Sight on the red pennant or the green light
so long as it's upward or onward. Or the Cross.

Signs (the Yahrzeit)

I thought I saw your peregrine
enter the bare tree at the back of my yard
and went for field glasses
so I could console you with a sighting.
If it was he, he's gone, and the bird
in my vision's a glossy grackle,
the first of the year.

This black fellow, single, is a sign of spring.
Soon a cortege of his kind will pace the grass
as if in tailcoats and their duller wives
will arrive.

All winter near sundown I've seen
hundreds of crows streaming
in the city-gray sky, marks
like graffiti of our non-dominion.
Sometimes alarm at their teeming
tinges my joy in their bold darks.

My fearless friend, always happier in the open,
alive to joy in any tree, bird, square of sky,
today your grief's not brushed away
by bud or wing. It's always the human
that holds terrors for you
and this black-letter day
marks the immoveable fast
when unseasonably fell,
far and forever, one of your nest.

Forbes Avenue Bridge

The high bridge carries a roadway out of town,
an earlier generation's pride and wonder,
emblem of man's ambition. From below
on the park path, it's an iron rainbow,

a sky that booms with ungiving thunder
above a shallow stream that gave no grace
to the promising son who did himself to death
choosing to break himself on the dusty path.

Above, the walker along the red-painted rail,
pausing, has distance and time to see
the ordained net,
the thick unconscious trees.

Walking across an ancient bridge in Spain,
midway I saw a saint, feet hidden in wax.
On the bridge between us can we build such a shrine
to consecrate a place where I flinch to look down?

And on this bare span conjure a blessed shape,
a braided cord to be lit by journeyers?
Mourner, comforter, relict—offer thanks
for the sad iron we walk over the gap.

Tough Cookie

In those two-by-two days
when the yoke chafed
when the mate
stopped pulling his weight
kicked over the traces
got plowed every night
you stayed with the narrative ark
cut dough into diamonds
leaving no leavings

now you're rerolling scraps
making the best of it
of the rest of it
tough cookie widowhood
or being left
or even leaving

some burdens seem heavier
when put down
the arm misses something when
you're shopping and lose
a package

even after twenty years
you zone out
driving a long way
turn to look back

Where's
      the baby?

My Hearing Aids

Curved like tiny shofars,
my hearing aids recall
their ancestor, the speaking trumpet.
They're yoked to clear casts
of my ears' voids, plastic ghosts.

My first hearing aid
was the indecent yellow-tinged pink
of my grandmother's girdle—
peach-color, once called *flesh*,
like her Shabbos chicken's flesh.

Hard plastic, torqued, on my palm
it looked like Francis Bacon's
tortured nude men, or an embryo.
An infant in reverse: umbilicus
that fed me music, voices, noise.

Some new year will I not hear
the shofar speak,
ram's horn of the ancestors
that calls to prayer, that I still hear
with shivery joy?

Sounded, it shattered walls
of stone or baked brick,
surely will pierce
my shuttered ear.

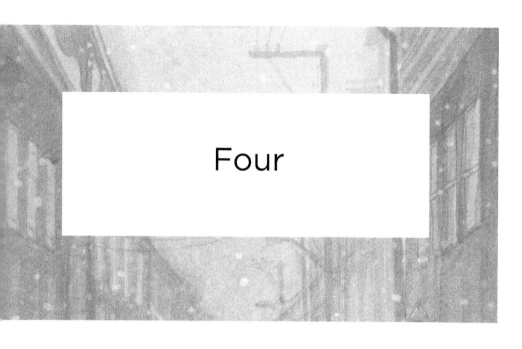

Four

What is that ripping sound in the air?

History tearing her petticoats.
—*Does she mourn then*
like us? Or care for the wounded?

No. Her darkened cloth summons armies,
covers complicit eyes, hangs rebels from lampposts,
tenderly wipes the asses of great men. Buy

her smile with thousands of men, with bombs,
with pyramids of masonry or skulls;
fan her with your manifesto. She

forgets all her lovers, her little children.
Do you remember Ustrashana, that great city?
Under sand. —*What is that light?*

Thousands reduced to ash for her pleasure,
to turn her step. History is tearing
her red, red petticoats, that sweep

peoples away like dust.
—*You are speaking of war, not History.*
What is History but war?
The rest is punctuation.

Suckling in Wartime

One summer Mama took me weekly by subway and bus
to high hushed rooms. My great-aunt lay in bed
her arms like spilled milk on the satin spread,
and if I played in the foyer quietly
and got a good report from Annie, the Negro maid,
Mama would take me to a shop of expensive lead
grenadiers, Trojans, and cavalry
to choose a figure for my Manhattan farm.
I ranged my fences, my collie and sheep,
on the floor that shook as the trucks went by on Nagle.
I raised and lowered the farmwife's articulate arm
to scatter feed all day to her tiny hens.

My little love, my son, as I suckled you
jets boomed above us. Green helicopters
brought their bagged harvest home.
I could have spent night and day in one motion,
one duty, one connection, a lead mother
in a land flat and dear, where the great trucks
rumbling by were too loud to sound…
but I must not shrink you down.

Dateline Nineveh

The penciled price was cheap when I,
a student, bought a black-letter page
from a world-chronicle in a dead language.

It came from an early book,
charmed me with difficult
crabbed lettering, artless illustration:

Playing-card kings. A city falling. Towers
and houses lean crookedly,
a belvedere gapes,

horrified mouth. On the peaked roof
of a substantial and doomed building, a cross,
though the picture is labeled *Babilon.*

A turret breaks cleanly, opening
like a Christmas cracker,
gift of a new order.

Thrift of the printing house
made one picture serve
for any city in its ruin,

Babylon, Nineveh, Rome,
like thrift of epic songs, psalms,
the repetitions of the defeated

that crack the towers open,
shuffle over and over
the playing cards for War, childhood's
monotonous game of chance.

I'm Vick's Dog

We're bred to fight,
fed to fight,
blooded, trained to fight,
hold on tight
till victory

and if we're chained,
some hanged or brained
who don't have heart enough,
the right stuff,
no guts, no glory.

We're hired, wired,
fired up to fight,
no fear.
We take ears.

Good stink
of men around
no candy asses
who drink from glasses
here
money passes
bottles clink
cheers sound.

We're
born to the pit
never out of it.

Nearer

All day our brilliant screens show without letup
hysterical screamers winning money prizes,
a woman sneering at another's getup,
boys doing jackass stunts in various guises,
in aspiration to become *well known.*
A reporter poses before a green setup
and picturesque, a foreign ruin rises.
A war somewhere, an earthquake. No surprises.

But images now, sent from a cellphone,
show kids you know shooting, shot, dead! Alone
on the sofa, God sleeps through these dull affairs,
this noise, while darling Pity watches Terror
caper and tap dance up and down the stairs.

Three Pointing Back

and thumb cocked ready.
Running around the empty lots.
Two shiny Dale Evans pistols came
with belt, holsters, red hat.
Origin story: big bang.
Blame blame blame.

A hand-me-down toy Colt
was better: dull gunmetal, big.
Loaded with Mom's
Prince Matchabelli powder,
it smoked. Blame blame.

A mother's son in Kevlar made a stand
with an AK-47, laid
three policemen down.
Pry my gun from my cold dead hand.
Blame blame blame.

Hate speech, talk radio, video game.
Salad shooter, cookie gun.
My hair dryer's not innocent.
Improvised explanatory devices. Blame
the way we live now.

When Roy Rogers shot, his aim true,
the bad guy, shocked, rubbed his hurt wrist, *Ow!*

Thumb on the Scale

Overnight yellow-green pollen
covered my car like a Rose Bowl float.
I drove it to Home Depot, wandered
among bedding plants, chose.

In the parking lot a man with bad teeth
came close, took out a handkerchief,
I don't want to see you drive it like this,
wiped part of the roof.

I gave him two quarters. He quit, complained,
I been here since 4:30 a.m. trying to make
four bucks. Haven't eaten in three days.
I didn't buy him pizza,

or make him a sandwich and drive back,
which would have said, *I believed your hustle,*
wouldn't have fed your real hungers.
In truth I forgot him.

A frantic buzz draws me out of the house.
Starlings' noisy young solicit care.
One bird has found a dumpster, emerges
to fill a yellow gape.

My black cat is out. When his eyes
watch a rabbit or robin
I shut him in the house. Now
I don't call him in.

A Photo of Jalen, Age 12, in a Batman Costume

Where did you learn to cross your arms, frown
(not frown, unsmile), forbidding like the Nation
of Islam guards I once saw break up
a feel-good meeting, accusing a respectable
Black councilman of luring boys in the park
back when an Urban League officer joked
*We don't talk about Black Power, just Dark
Strength?* The councilman had brought his little daughter,
dressed in ruffled pink, left with her in a hurry.

Your first mother and father gone, like Bruce
Wayne's. To avenge the living dead, the self-
murdered living, the gone, the best revenge
is living well, and boy, if I may call you boy,
live well. Live long. A paper I just read
says, *"disarming mechanisms"... that signal
warmth, humility, or deference—
can lead to greater power and success
among minorities by making them appear less
threatening and adversarial to dominant groups.*

Sure, we get that, Smile, smile, smile,
unfold those arms, sit (do you have to be
so tall?) but be ready to jump through hoops.
Say *yes, sir* when the officers stop you
for the fourteenth time, looking
for somebody lighter than you, shorter than you,
or on spec: your tail-light's cracked, you fail
to maintain lane, you're Driving While Black.

Say *no* when somebody's girlfriend
leans into you in a bar. No, say nothing,
No might offend, *Yes* will offend. To be safer
avoid the bar, women, luxury cars, hoodies,
caps—or keep them to doff to the dominant—

and playful gang signs. Go out for track
but don't run cross-country.

Did I tell you, you look terrific, I like the way
you look? With the nerd glasses that you need
to read and build with Legos, with your wide
smile and as Batman too: Proud, manly,
though I'd rather see you without the mask.

Five

The Nonpregnant Uterus Is the Size of a Fist

and is all muscle. It's *like an inverted*
pear in a bowl. Nice. The pregnant uterus distends
to the size of a universe. Mine did, twice.

The first big bang: you were clenched
like a dime, a sixpence, a marble, then
a big boy, squeezed, released, lost

from my fist into air, but clutched
to my chest, where the heart, regular fellow
and famous, beats on the bars. He's the size

of a fist too, muscle too, something to do
with blood, but less spontaneous. You
kept expanding, grew clouds, missing matter,

grew dark, slipped my grip. Slept days,
watched nights. Watched a bowl of starred sky,
grew an appetite for southern objects.

These fists still grasp for you, clasp,
have blind black holes for you, not hollows,
though you've moved beyond, to the clouds
of Magellan, to galaxies far, swirling and barred.

Kinnehara

With a picture of his grandchild
my brother writes, *Don't you love
that toothless smile?* Pride,
shaded with self-mockery.
Not that I'd take umbrage,
I've no grandchild, but I'm inside
the warmth, his is my own.

I think how my first son,
when our father's brother
leaned down and saluted him
in his first Yiddish,
Vos is naias?
toothlessly laughed, his first laugh.

That uncle, a flier, so handsome
that women, girls then and grandmothers now,
remember him, lives—feels the tooth
of cancer at his liver, yesterday
post-surgery was weaned
from a respirator—breathes
on his own, but how long?
The spots are everywhere,
carried in his blood.

My first son's almost forty,
the tongue my father and grandmother spoke
lost to me, few words left:
a *hop-la* when the baby's raised up,
swung high and a phrase—
Kein ayn ha-ra (my mother says,
Don't give me a canary) —
to ward off the Evil One
when the toothless, wide-eyed,
blessed baby's praised.

The Two

Behind his lids a pale round against the dark
and a smaller, dazzling crescent: the new moon
with the old in its arms, or a growing infant
head downward, in its sac.

When they'd first learned she was pregnant,
he had an impossible deadline, stayed
in the office, pillowed his head on his desk,
woke at dawn, looked out: *Earth*

has not anything to show more fair,
then saw with alarm on the roof of the chemistry building,
two figures, by their different heights
a mother and child. *What are they doing there,*

it's dangerous! Masts around them, exhausts,
ventilator ducts and prey to unpredictable winds.

But the two that caught his eye were standpipes,
unthreatened, furniture of the building.
Yet his panic heartbeat continued for a while.

For Anne, Pregnant, on the Anniversary of the Moon Landing

For eight months you've been a sea
with an island continent,
an imperial nation
with one citizen tenderly held—
not subject but sovereign
though soon to be expelled.

Meanwhile, to him
according to his needs—
you're his all: chamber
and chamber orchestra, grocery,
and—let it be said—
his chamber pot, though he's pure.

A little given to piracy,
he exacts tribute from your bones,
taxes your blood,
softens your joinery
so your hips waddle
as you cradle him.

In this ninth month we begin
to count our unhatched chick,
finding it difficult
to live in the moment
when a coming moment
will be so momentous

(not forgetting the hen,
your health, your strength):
we count down toward the launch
from the mother ship,
how the great valve of you will shudder
and thrust him, our breath

held for his awful balancing
between the worlds, from the moony
secure black-and-white one
we've seen on a sonogram,
where no wind blows,
to our ruddy, noisy, and too-bloody earth.

The Milk Comes In

On the third day of suckling, you're engorged.
Your breasts, never before your best feature,
are large and are stone, from which this small
never-before-seen creature can get—not blood,
but the only humor of the body not salt.
Taste a drop.

Your man may enjoy this mammary maximum
but the momentary miracle isn't for him.
You comprehend him better now,
the unwilled tides of his sex,
as briefly you're phallic, hard as a rock.
How little we are ruled by the neocortex
when a wee cry, a peep, calls forth
feeling, leakage, a flood,
the let-down reflex.

You may weep at the same time,
as if you didn't exude fluid enough—
rusty blood's still coming, yours,
the plush lining that cushioned the child
and that dark red organ that you shared,
that left you behind. An animal mother
would turn and eat it. Maybe the doctor
showed it to you, wonderful as it is,
but it had no future, you faced toward your sun.

Fear not, your slack belly will contract,
you'll stop leaking blood and tears.
Allow yourself to feel pleasure,
along with the possible cracked
nipple. Lean your cheek against the silk
of his skin. Another nine months and this act
will have some teeth in it.

For an Infant Refusing To Be Swaddled

We would protect you against cold and heat.
We would protect you against dirt and danger,
against pests and pestilence. Against wild creatures
and against dear pets who might savage you
we would protect you. Against your own nature
that kicks against the binding blanket,
that may someday hurtle down stairs,
leap at windows, care for strangers we hate,
dare perilous new countries, we would protect you.

We would prevent your tears.
We would nurse you, rock you,
chant endearments, explain
that the monsters are all dead
though the monsters are not dead:
some may be reared a half-mile off, go to your school.
Some, we know, enter children with tools,
set fire to houses (we will pretend to you
that houses are safe) with bombs and pointed missiles.

We will keep pointed missiles from you,
toy guns, teach you that blocks are for building,
not for throwing at the cat.
We will spread your bread with sweetness,
cut it into triangles to fit your small mouth,
conceal from you that the meat you eat
comes from woolly lambs and glittering fish
like the ones in your books, keep from you
the knowledge that other children
shrivel in want and shiver in cold.

We would defend you against each other,
against ourselves. We who were once

truthful and brave, who strode out against armies
now tremble to read the news.
We who were just, who shared, hoard and save.

We cut the world small now, spread it with sweetness
because you are ours, because you are our sweetness.

All Souls' Day, Being Anne's Birthday

all hallows' past
all souls' day follows
dark laps at day
fallowtime

souls
journey in the wind

you call
joyous
to tell

cold pressure on your belly
a shadow of sound
pierced the veil

of flesh
foretold
female birth
in spring

First Day of School

He cried. Not just at the door, but in the Welcome Circle.
Smiles, songs, didn't console him.
As if he foresaw twelve years of sitting,
of alphabetical order.

The cage of the calendar, ruled lines,
the grid of routines, in exchange
for reading and writing.
For the marching beads of multiplication.

Alarms, zippers, packed lunches,
for maps, charts, string, paste, paint.

I remember a film of two women in the Amazon,
chatting on a sleeping platform.
Their people, a small group,
of interest to the documentarian.
It's said they have no concept of number.

Below the women, a child of four or so,
playing with a machete. The boy cried out.
He'd dropped the knife. One woman
reached down for it, handed it back to him,
continued her conversation.

For houses, cars, money, tamed animals.

Six

To a Nighthawk

Flutterling, over the square bulk of buildings
I hear your call, vibration of a slack string,
look up from hurry over the cracks
of a city street where we oblivious dart
from task to task.

                     Below, streetlights on,
it's dusk, while your moth flurry
makes white marks on a sky still light.

You say to us, dark continues its life, teems as we sleep
and may I see, day sleeper, your endpaper wings
folded in rest on a roof among vents and pipes.
What dreams among the unloved skyscape of utility?

Let me gape like you, gate-mouthed moth-gathering bird,
like the great whale whelming krill,
swallow the world before me,
find in the stars the faint companion of Alcor,
take all in, dry and wet, dawn and dark.

Downward

Cold rain paves the path
with gold leaves, calls
to mind the future:
fall of snow. Must
every bright thing
fall, all wither, freeze,
erase our swept paths,
our steps?

How to become
like the earth,
that feels a fall
as a drawing down,
the way a lover's face
is drawn down? How
to get that unjudging appetite—
inward, inward—dust,
petals, bedsprings,
water silvered with oil?

Come: the stinking grizzled
man carrying a plank,
the sixteen-year-old
stricken in the stadium,
millions of thistle seeds,
sparrows, meteorites.
...to draw the sun a little
and the moon much.

John of the Lamp

John of the lamp, poor fellow,
you're quite unstrung.
Cat or rat's got your tongue.
Your guts are yellow,
your wide grin is hollow.

Summon the young
to a portal they, callow,
don't fear, like us who've clung
to life so long.

Tomorrow your tallowy
remains will be flung
to the compost heap.
You'll triumph, though:

when next year
a green vine will creep
over the bordered lawn
to say you were here.

Foggy Morning Breakdown

fog drops a wooly shawl over
November's shabby shoulders

kind as the Vaseline
daubed on camera lenses

for aging beauties
(gauze for menopause)

I want to move from sleep
to sleep   alone

curl up   a pill bug
creep   into gray fleece

but the backslapping sun's
opening a hole

like a run in a pair of tights
and   it's going to be another

high-definition day
sharp and loud

he's taking my scarf   my coat
holding up a magnifying mirror

reminding me I'm due
on the morning show

to chat with the anchorwoman
Sally Death

Untrimmed

Clear your greens out of the house by Twelfth Night,
we've heard, or devils will get into them.

The naked Christmas trees along the curb
show green and perfect, only fallen.

They lean, tops waiting to be spun,
or point like arrows. There must be lore

to read their fresh-sawn ends, like tea leaves
or Tarot, to tell the new year's luck.

A plastic shroud conceals one tree,
the only white this snowless day.

The scouring wind lifts it and lets it drop
as breath lifts and lets drop a sheeted sleeper's breast.

Candlemas Day

Saint of the Day, an app
available for iPhone,
today brings up "Presentation
of the Lord."

Is there no hermit saint for today,
no prophet who dwelt underground?
Yesterday St. Brigid, tomorrow
St. Blaise, who lived peaceably
with bears and wolves but among men
was torn with iron combs.

Saint Groundhog, Saint Woodchuck,
better known than Candlemas,
is patron of dormancy, of earth,
slow-moving, furred, patient, heavy.
Light stays a little longer now with us,
who tunnel in cold and dark for half the year.
The year turns—but no seer
persuades that winter ever ends in March.

The Beauty

To the far corner
of the small ill-tended yard
I carried dry stems for compost.
I found, obscure, a rose of sharon,
roots in the heap, self-sown.

The blooms' pure white
flared in the near dark,
unmarked with the blue-red bee
that most of her kind bear,
Sacred Heart, or menstrual blot.

I thrust a spade
into the hard earth,
meaning to transplant her
into the light.
She stood obstinate, her own.

Pucelle, I lay sticks at your feet
as if to feed a fire.
They strengthen you.
Unbled puella,
you flower like a daughter
while I your mother wither.

The Tick

Ixodes doesn't calculate
or think of its career
which is, in fact, complex:
from mouse to deer
to pubic hair. It simply waits
and does what's next:
which may be me or you.

The tick is all desire. Fear
it. It knows not what it does
but blood's what it pursues.
Ixodes' licks
may leave you with the blues.
Once it connects, it sticks.

Sepia officinalis

Something is whetting a blade
as your canary whets its beak
on a cuttlefish bone.

The bird drinks the water,
the yellow bird eats the seed
that you place with tender care.

Something untender is whetting
a blade for our joys, something
as ignorant of our hearts

as we of the cuttlefish,
who stretches two arms to its mate
in the sea, who makes black ink,

the soft, great-eyed cuttlefish
with its bony beak.

Acknowledgments

"At Spuyten Duyvil" appeared in *Paterson Literary Review, 43.*

"By the Sink" appeared in *Uppagus* (uppagus.com), *2.*

"Comfort Zone" appeared in *Rune,* 2011.

"Downward" appeared in *Coal Hill Review* (coalhillreview.com), September 2010.

"Experiment in Living" and "Seconds and Irregulars" appeared in *Vox Populi* (voxpopulisphere.com).

"Flamenco Dancer in White" appeared in *Fission of Form,* Pittsburgh Society of Sculptors, 2009.

"Glove Song" appeared in *Eating Her Wedding Dress: A Collection of Clothing Poems,* E. Foos, V. Katsarou, and R. O'Toole, eds. Princeton, NJ: Ragged Sky Press, 2009.

"I'm Vick's Dog" appeared in *The Main Street Rag, 21,* Winter 2016.

"First Day of School," "In Junior High School I Was Voted Most Cheerful," "Like Love," and "The Tick" appeared in *U.S. 1 Worksheets,* various issues.

"Line of Beauty" appeared in *The Intima: a Journal of Narrative Medicine* (theintima.org), Spring 2015.

"My Husband Buys Cheese at Pennsylvania Macaroni Co." appeared in *The Strip!,* Fall 2013.

"Second-Hand Hat" appeared in *Voices in the Attic, XXI.* Pittsburgh: Carlow University.

"Skyfall" appeared in *Pittsburgh Poetry Review, 1.*

"Sustainability" appeared in *Hawk and Handsaw: A Journal of Creative Sustainability, 1.*

"Three Pointing Back" appeared in *White Gardenia Poetry Press,* (romellakitch.wordpress.com), July 2012.

CPSIA information can be obtained at www.ICGtesting.com
Printed in the USA
BVOW08s2012070516

447151BV00001B/3/P